THE ULTIMATE FISHING

LOG BOOK

THE ESSENTIAL ACCESSORY FOR THE TACKLE BOX

M. PREFONTAINE

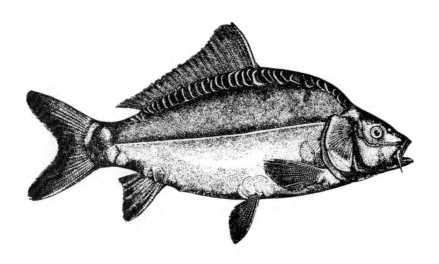

PUBLISHED BY MP PUBLISHING

NAME: ....

....

ADDRESS: ....

....

....

....

....

PHONE: ....

MOBILE: ....

NOTES: ....

....

....

....

....

....

DATE: ....

LOCATION: ....

HOURS FISHED: ....

DAY: ....

WATER: ....

BEST TIMES: ....

PEOPLE FISHED WITH: ....

WEATHER (AM): ....

WEATHER (PM): ....

AIR TEMP: ....   WATER TEMP: ....

AIR TEMP: ....   WATER TEMP: ....

SWIM: ....

RIG: ....

NOTES: ....

MOON: ●◑◐◒○

SPECIES	BAIT	TIME	WEIGHT	LENGTH	COMMENTS

SPECIES CAUGHT:

TOTAL FISH CAUGHT:

DATE:	LOCATION:	HOURS FISHED:
DAY:	WATER:	BEST TIMES:

PEOPLE FISHED WITH:

WEATHER (AM):	WEATHER (PM):
AIR TEMP: WATER TEMP:	AIR TEMP: WATER TEMP:

SWIM:	RIG:

NOTES:

MOON: ● ◖ ◖ ◖ ◯

SPECIES	BAIT	TIME	WEIGHT	LENGTH	COMMENTS

SPECIES CAUGHT:

....

TOTAL FISH CAUGHT:

....

DATE:	LOCATION:	HOURS FISHED:
DAY:	WATER:	BEST TIMES:

PEOPLE FISHED WITH:

WEATHER (AM):	WEATHER (PM):
AIR TEMP: WATER TEMP:	AIR TEMP: WATER TEMP:

SWIM:	RIG:

NOTES:

MOON: ●◖◖◖◖○

SPECIES	BAIT	TIME	WEIGHT	LENGTH	COMMENTS

SPECIES CAUGHT:

TOTAL FISH CAUGHT:

DATE:	LOCATION:	HOURS FISHED:
DAY:	WATER:	BEST TIMES:

PEOPLE FISHED WITH:

WEATHER (AM):	WEATHER (PM):
AIR TEMP: WATER TEMP:	AIR TEMP: WATER TEMP:

SWIM:	RIG:

NOTES:

MOON:

SPECIES	BAIT	TIME	WEIGHT	LENGTH	COMMENTS

SPECIES CAUGHT:

TOTAL FISH CAUGHT:

DATE: .... LOCATION: .... HOURS FISHED:
....
....

DAY: .... WATER: .... BEST TIMES: ....
....
....

PEOPLE FISHED WITH: ....
....
....

WEATHER (AM): .... WEATHER (PM): ....
....
....
....

AIR TEMP: WATER TEMP: AIR TEMP: WATER TEMP:
....

SWIM: .... RIG: ....
....
....

NOTES: ....   MOON: ●◗◖◗○
....
....
....
....
....

SPECIES	BAIT	TIME	WEIGHT	LENGTH	COMMENTS

SPECIES CAUGHT:

TOTAL FISH CAUGHT:

DATE:	LOCATION:	HOURS FISHED: ....
....	....	....
DAY:	WATER:	BEST TIMES: ....

PEOPLE FISHED WITH: ....
....
....

| WEATHER (AM): .... | WEATHER (PM): .... |
| AIR TEMP: WATER TEMP: .... | AIR TEMP: WATER TEMP: .... |

| SWIM: .... | RIG: .... |

NOTES: ....

MOON: ● ◖ ◖ ◗ ○

....
....
....
....
....

SPECIES	BAIT	TIME	WEIGHT	LENGTH	COMMENTS

SPECIES CAUGHT:

TOTAL FISH CAUGHT:

| DATE: .... | LOCATION: .... | HOURS FISHED: |
| DAY: .... | WATER: .... | BEST TIMES: .... |

PEOPLE FISHED WITH: ....

WEATHER (AM): ....

WEATHER (PM): ....

AIR TEMP: ....   WATER TEMP: ....

AIR TEMP: ....   WATER TEMP: ....

SWIM: ....

RIG: ....

NOTES: ....

MOON: ● ◗ ◖ ☾ ○

SPECIES	BAIT	TIME	WEIGHT	LENGTH	COMMENTS

SPECIES CAUGHT:

TOTAL FISH CAUGHT:

DATE: ....

LOCATION: ....

HOURS FISHED: ....

DAY: ....

WATER: ....

BEST TIMES: ....

PEOPLE FISHED WITH: ....

WEATHER (AM): ....

WEATHER (PM): ....

AIR TEMP: .... **WATER TEMP:** ....

AIR TEMP: .... **WATER TEMP:** ....

SWIM: ....

RIG: ....

NOTES: ....

MOON: ● ◗ ◖ ◑ ○

SPECIES	BAIT	TIME	WEIGHT	LENGTH	COMMENTS

SPECIES CAUGHT:

TOTAL FISH CAUGHT:

DATE:	LOCATION:	HOURS FISHED:
DAY:	WATER:	BEST TIMES:

PEOPLE FISHED WITH:

WEATHER (AM):	WEATHER (PM):
AIR TEMP: WATER TEMP:	AIR TEMP: WATER TEMP:

SWIM:	RIG:

NOTES:

MOON:

SPECIES	BAIT	TIME	WEIGHT	LENGTH	COMMENTS

SPECIES CAUGHT:

....

TOTAL FISH CAUGHT:

....

DATE:	LOCATION:	HOURS FISHED:
....		....
....	....	....
DAY:	WATER:	BEST TIMES: ....
....	....	....
....	....	....

PEOPLE FISHED WITH: ....
....
....

WEATHER (AM):	WEATHER (PM): ....
....	....
....	....
....	....
AIR TEMP: WATER TEMP:	AIR TEMP: WATER TEMP:
....	....

SWIM:	RIG: ....
....	....
....	....

NOTES: ....   MOON: ● ◐ ◑ ☾ ○
....
....
....
....
....

SPECIES	BAIT	TIME	WEIGHT	LENGTH	COMMENTS

SPECIES CAUGHT:

....

TOTAL FISH CAUGHT:

....

DATE:	LOCATION:	HOURS FISHED:
DAY:	WATER:	BEST TIMES:

PEOPLE FISHED WITH:

WEATHER (AM):	WEATHER (PM):
AIR TEMP: WATER TEMP:	AIR TEMP: WATER TEMP:

SWIM:	RIG:

NOTES: | MOON: ● ◖ ◖ ◗ ○

SPECIES	BAIT	TIME	WEIGHT	LENGTH	COMMENTS

SPECIES CAUGHT:

....

TOTAL FISH CAUGHT:

....

DATE:	LOCATION:	HOURS FISHED:
....	....	....
....	....	....
DAY:	WATER:	BEST TIMES: ....
....	....	....
....	....	....

PEOPLE FISHED WITH: ....
....
....

WEATHER (AM):	WEATHER (PM): ....
....	....
....	....
....	....
AIR TEMP: WATER TEMP:	AIR TEMP: WATER TEMP:
....	....

SWIM:	RIG: ....
....	....
....	....

NOTES: ....   **MOON:** ● ◑ ◐ ◗ ○
....
....
....
....
....

SPECIES	BAIT	TIME	WEIGHT	LENGTH	COMMENTS

SPECIES CAUGHT:
....

TOTAL FISH CAUGHT:
....

| DATE: .... | LOCATION: .... | HOURS FISHED: |
| DAY: .... | WATER: .... | BEST TIMES: .... |

PEOPLE FISHED WITH: ....
....
....

| WEATHER (AM): .... | WEATHER (PM): .... |
| AIR TEMP: WATER TEMP: | AIR TEMP: WATER TEMP: |

| SWIM: .... | RIG: .... |

NOTES: ....

MOON: ● ◗ ◖ ☾ ○

SPECIES	BAIT	TIME	WEIGHT	LENGTH	COMMENTS

SPECIES CAUGHT:
....

TOTAL FISH CAUGHT:
....

DATE:	LOCATION:	HOURS FISHED:
DAY:	WATER:	BEST TIMES:

PEOPLE FISHED WITH:

WEATHER (AM):	WEATHER (PM):
AIR TEMP: WATER TEMP:	AIR TEMP: WATER TEMP:

SWIM:	RIG:

NOTES:

MOON:

SPECIES	BAIT	TIME	WEIGHT	LENGTH	COMMENTS

SPECIES CAUGHT:

....

TOTAL FISH CAUGHT:

....

| DATE: .... | LOCATION: .... | HOURS FISHED: .... |
| DAY: .... | WATER: .... | BEST TIMES: .... |

PEOPLE FISHED WITH: ....
....
....

WEATHER (AM):	WEATHER (PM): ....
AIR TEMP: WATER TEMP:	AIR TEMP: WATER TEMP:
....	....

| SWIM: .... | RIG: .... |

NOTES: ....

MOON: ● ◐ ◑ ☾ ○

....
....
....
....

SPECIES	BAIT	TIME	WEIGHT	LENGTH	COMMENTS

SPECIES CAUGHT:
....

TOTAL FISH CAUGHT:
....

DATE:	LOCATION:	HOURS FISHED:
....		....
....		....
DAY:	WATER:	BEST TIMES: ....
....		....
....		....

PEOPLE FISHED WITH: ....
....
....

WEATHER (AM):	WEATHER (PM): ....
....	....
....	....
....	....
AIR TEMP: WATER TEMP:	AIR TEMP: WATER TEMP:
....	....

SWIM:	RIG: ....
....	....
....	....

NOTES: ....

MOON: ● ◗ ◗ ☾ ○

....
....
....
....
....

SPECIES	BAIT	TIME	WEIGHT	LENGTH	COMMENTS

SPECIES CAUGHT:

TOTAL FISH CAUGHT:

DATE:	LOCATION:	HOURS FISHED:
....	....	....
....	....	....
DAY:	WATER:	BEST TIMES: ....
....	....	....
....	....	....

PEOPLE FISHED WITH: ....
....
....

WEATHER (AM):	WEATHER (PM): ....
....	....
....	....
....	....
AIR TEMP: WATER TEMP:	AIR TEMP: WATER TEMP:
....	....

SWIM:	RIG: ....
....	....
....	....

| NOTES: .... | MOON: ● ◑ ◐ ☾ ○ |

....
....
....
....
....

SPECIES	BAIT	TIME	WEIGHT	LENGTH	COMMENTS

SPECIES CAUGHT:
....

TOTAL FISH CAUGHT:
....

DATE:	LOCATION:	HOURS FISHED:
....	....	....
....	....	....
DAY:	WATER:	BEST TIMES: ....
....	....	....
....	....	....

PEOPLE FISHED WITH: ....
....
....

WEATHER (AM):	WEATHER (PM): ....
....	....
....	....
....	
AIR TEMP: WATER TEMP:	AIR TEMP: WATER TEMP:
....	....

SWIM:	RIG: ....
....	....
....	

NOTES: ....

MOON: ● ◗ ◖ ☾ ○

....
....
....
....
....

SPECIES	BAIT	TIME	WEIGHT	LENGTH	COMMENTS

SPECIES CAUGHT:

TOTAL FISH CAUGHT:

DATE:	LOCATION:	HOURS FISHED:
....	....	....
....	....	....
DAY:	WATER:	BEST TIMES: ....
....	....	....
....	....	....

PEOPLE FISHED WITH: ....
....
....

WEATHER (AM):	WEATHER (PM): ....
....	....
....	....
....	....
AIR TEMP: WATER TEMP:	AIR TEMP: WATER TEMP:
....	....

SWIM:	RIG: ....
....	....
....	....

| NOTES: .... | MOON: ● ◗ ◖ ☾ ○ |

....
....
....
....
....

SPECIES	BAIT	TIME	WEIGHT	LENGTH	COMMENTS

SPECIES CAUGHT:

....

TOTAL FISH CAUGHT:

....

| DATE: .... | LOCATION: .... | HOURS FISHED: |
| DAY: .... | WATER: .... | BEST TIMES: .... |

PEOPLE FISHED WITH: ....

| WEATHER (AM): .... | WEATHER (PM): .... |

| AIR TEMP: | WATER TEMP: | AIR TEMP: | WATER TEMP: |
| .... | .... | .... | .... |

| SWIM: .... | RIG: .... |

| NOTES: .... | MOON: ● ◖ ◗ ☾ ○ |

SPECIES	BAIT	TIME	WEIGHT	LENGTH	COMMENTS

SPECIES CAUGHT:

TOTAL FISH CAUGHT:

DATE:	LOCATION:	HOURS FISHED:
DAY:	WATER:	BEST TIMES:

PEOPLE FISHED WITH:

WEATHER (AM):	WEATHER (PM):
AIR TEMP: WATER TEMP:	AIR TEMP: WATER TEMP:

SWIM:	RIG:

NOTES:

MOON: ● ◐ ◑ ◗ ○

SPECIES	BAIT	TIME	WEIGHT	LENGTH	COMMENTS

SPECIES CAUGHT:

TOTAL FISH CAUGHT:

DATE:	LOCATION:	HOURS FISHED:
....	....	....
....	....	....

DAY:	WATER:	BEST TIMES: ....
....	....	....
....	....	....

PEOPLE FISHED WITH: ....
....
....

WEATHER (AM):	WEATHER (PM): ....
....	....
....	....
....	
AIR TEMP: WATER TEMP:	AIR TEMP: WATER TEMP:
....	....

SWIM:	RIG: ....
....	....
....	....

NOTES: ....   MOON: ● ◐ ◑ ☽ ○
....
....
....
....
....

SPECIES	BAIT	TIME	WEIGHT	LENGTH	COMMENTS

SPECIES CAUGHT:

TOTAL FISH CAUGHT:

DATE:	LOCATION:	HOURS FISHED:
DAY:	WATER:	BEST TIMES:

PEOPLE FISHED WITH:

WEATHER (AM):	WEATHER (PM):
AIR TEMP: WATER TEMP:	AIR TEMP: WATER TEMP:

SWIM:	RIG:

NOTES:

MOON:

SPECIES	BAIT	TIME	WEIGHT	LENGTH	COMMENTS

SPECIES CAUGHT:

TOTAL FISH CAUGHT:

DATE:	LOCATION:	HOURS FISHED:
DAY:	WATER:	BEST TIMES:

PEOPLE FISHED WITH:

WEATHER (AM):	WEATHER (PM):
AIR TEMP: WATER TEMP:	AIR TEMP: WATER TEMP:

SWIM:	RIG:

NOTES:

MOON:

SPECIES	BAIT	TIME	WEIGHT	LENGTH	COMMENTS

SPECIES CAUGHT:

TOTAL FISH CAUGHT:

DATE:	LOCATION:	HOURS FISHED:
....	....	....
....	....	....
DAY:	WATER:	BEST TIMES: ....
....	....	....
....	....	....

PEOPLE FISHED WITH: ....
....
....

WEATHER (AM):	WEATHER (PM): ....
....	....
....	....
....	....
AIR TEMP: WATER TEMP:	AIR TEMP: WATER TEMP:
....	....

SWIM:	RIG: ....
....	....
....	....

NOTES: .... MOON: ● ◐ ◑ ☾ ○
....
....
....
....
....

SPECIES	BAIT	TIME	WEIGHT	LENGTH	COMMENTS

SPECIES CAUGHT:
....

TOTAL FISH CAUGHT:
....

DATE:	LOCATION:	HOURS FISHED:
....	....	....
....	....	....
DAY:	WATER:	BEST TIMES: ....
....	....	....
....	....	....

PEOPLE FISHED WITH: ....
....
....

WEATHER (AM):	WEATHER (PM): ....
....	....
....	....
....	....
AIR TEMP: WATER TEMP:	AIR TEMP: WATER TEMP:
....	....

SWIM:	RIG: ....
....	....
....	....

NOTES: ....

MOON: ● ◑ ◐ ◗ ○

....
....
....
....
....

SPECIES	BAIT	TIME	WEIGHT	LENGTH	COMMENTS

SPECIES CAUGHT:

TOTAL FISH CAUGHT:

DATE: .... LOCATION: .... HOURS FISHED:
....
....

DAY: .... WATER: .... BEST TIMES: ....
....
....

PEOPLE FISHED WITH: ....
....
....

WEATHER (AM): .... WEATHER (PM): ....
....
....
....

AIR TEMP: WATER TEMP: AIR TEMP: WATER TEMP:
....

SWIM: .... RIG: ....
....
....

NOTES: .... MOON: ● ☾ ☾ ☾ ○
....
....
....
....
....

SPECIES	BAIT	TIME	WEIGHT	LENGTH	COMMENTS

SPECIES CAUGHT:

TOTAL FISH CAUGHT:

DATE:	LOCATION:	HOURS FISHED:
....	....	....
....	....	....
DAY:	WATER:	BEST TIMES: ....
....	....	....
....	....	....

PEOPLE FISHED WITH: ....
....
....

WEATHER (AM):	WEATHER (PM): ....
....	....
....	....
....	....
AIR TEMP: WATER TEMP:	AIR TEMP: WATER TEMP:
....	....

SWIM:	RIG: ....
....	
....	

NOTES: ....   MOON: ● ◐ ◑ ☽ ○
....
....
....
....
....

SPECIES	BAIT	TIME	WEIGHT	LENGTH	COMMENTS

SPECIES CAUGHT:

....

TOTAL FISH CAUGHT:

....

DATE:	LOCATION:	HOURS FISHED:
....	....	....
....	....	....
DAY:	WATER:	BEST TIMES: ....
....	....	....
....	....	....

PEOPLE FISHED WITH: ....
....
....

WEATHER (AM):	WEATHER (PM): ....
....	....
....	....
....	....
AIR TEMP: WATER TEMP:	AIR TEMP: WATER TEMP:
....	....

SWIM:	RIG: ....
....	....
....	....

NOTES: ....   MOON: ● ◐ ◑ ☾ ○
....
....
....
....
....

SPECIES	BAIT	TIME	WEIGHT	LENGTH	COMMENTS

SPECIES CAUGHT:
....

TOTAL FISH CAUGHT:
....

DATE: .... LOCATION: .... HOURS FISHED:
....
....

DAY: .... WATER: .... BEST TIMES: ....
....
....

PEOPLE FISHED WITH: ....
....
....

WEATHER (AM): .... WEATHER (PM): ....
....
....
....

AIR TEMP: WATER TEMP: AIR TEMP: WATER TEMP:
....

SWIM: .... RIG: ....
....
....

NOTES: .... MOON: ● ◗ ◖ ☾ ○
....
....
....
....
....

SPECIES	BAIT	TIME	WEIGHT	LENGTH	COMMENTS

SPECIES CAUGHT:

TOTAL FISH CAUGHT:

DATE:	LOCATION:	HOURS FISHED:
....	....	....
DAY:	WATER:	BEST TIMES: ....
....	....	....

PEOPLE FISHED WITH: ....
....
....

WEATHER (AM):	WEATHER (PM): ....
....	....
....	....
....	....
AIR TEMP: WATER TEMP:	AIR TEMP: WATER TEMP:
....	....

SWIM:	RIG: ....
....	....
....	....

NOTES: ....   MOON: ● ◗ ◖ ☾ ○
....
....
....
....

SPECIES	BAIT	TIME	WEIGHT	LENGTH	COMMENTS

SPECIES CAUGHT:

TOTAL FISH CAUGHT:

DATE:	LOCATION:	HOURS FISHED:
....	....	....
....	....	....
DAY:	WATER:	BEST TIMES: ....
....	....	....
....	....	....

PEOPLE FISHED WITH: ....
....
....

WEATHER (AM):	WEATHER (PM): ....
....	....
....	....
....	....
AIR TEMP: WATER TEMP:	AIR TEMP: WATER TEMP:
....	....

SWIM:	RIG: ....
....	....
....	....

| NOTES: .... | MOON: ● ◐ ◑ ☾ ○ |

....
....
....
....
....

SPECIES	BAIT	TIME	WEIGHT	LENGTH	COMMENTS

SPECIES CAUGHT:

....

TOTAL FISH CAUGHT:

....

DATE:	LOCATION:	HOURS FISHED:
....	....	....
....	....	....
DAY:	WATER:	BEST TIMES: ....
....	....	....
....	....	....

PEOPLE FISHED WITH: ....
....
....

WEATHER (AM):	WEATHER (PM): ....
....	....
....	....
....	....
AIR TEMP: WATER TEMP:	AIR TEMP: WATER TEMP:
....	....

SWIM:	RIG: ....
....	....
....	....

NOTES: ....   MOON: ● ◗ ◖ ☾ ○
....
....
....
....
....

SPECIES	BAIT	TIME	WEIGHT	LENGTH	COMMENTS

SPECIES CAUGHT:

TOTAL FISH CAUGHT:

| DATE: .... | LOCATION: .... | HOURS FISHED: .... |
| DAY: .... | WATER: .... | BEST TIMES: .... |

PEOPLE FISHED WITH: ....
....
....

| WEATHER (AM): .... | WEATHER (PM): .... |
| AIR TEMP: WATER TEMP: .... | AIR TEMP: WATER TEMP: .... |

| SWIM: .... | RIG: .... |

NOTES: ....

MOON: ● ◑ ◐ ☾ ○

....
....
....
....
....

SPECIES	BAIT	TIME	WEIGHT	LENGTH	COMMENTS

SPECIES CAUGHT:

....

TOTAL FISH CAUGHT:

....

DATE: .... | LOCATION: .... | HOURS FISHED:

DAY: .... | WATER: .... | BEST TIMES: ....

PEOPLE FISHED WITH: ....

WEATHER (AM): .... | WEATHER (PM): ....

AIR TEMP: WATER TEMP: | AIR TEMP: WATER TEMP:

SWIM: .... | RIG: ....

NOTES: .... | MOON: ● ◗ ◖ ☾ ○

SPECIES	BAIT	TIME	WEIGHT	LENGTH	COMMENTS

SPECIES CAUGHT:

....

TOTAL FISH CAUGHT:

....

DATE: .... LOCATION: .... HOURS FISHED: ....
....
....

DAY: .... WATER: .... BEST TIMES: ....
....
....

PEOPLE FISHED WITH: ....
....
....

WEATHER (AM): .... WEATHER (PM): ....
....
....
....

AIR TEMP: WATER TEMP: AIR TEMP: WATER TEMP:
....

SWIM: .... RIG: ....
....
....

NOTES: .... MOON: ● ◑ ◐ ◔ ○
....
....
....
....

SPECIES	BAIT	TIME	WEIGHT	LENGTH	COMMENTS

SPECIES CAUGHT:

TOTAL FISH CAUGHT:

DATE: .... LOCATION: .... HOURS FISHED:
....
....

DAY: .... WATER: .... BEST TIMES: ....
....
....

PEOPLE FISHED WITH: ....
....
....

WEATHER (AM): .... WEATHER (PM): ....
....
....
....

AIR TEMP: WATER TEMP: AIR TEMP: WATER TEMP:
....

SWIM: .... RIG: ....
....
....

NOTES: .... MOON:
....
....
....
....
....

SPECIES	BAIT	TIME	WEIGHT	LENGTH	COMMENTS

SPECIES CAUGHT:

....

TOTAL FISH CAUGHT:

....

DATE:	LOCATION:	HOURS FISHED:
....	....	....
....	....	....
DAY:	WATER:	BEST TIMES: ....
....	....	....
....	....	....

PEOPLE FISHED WITH: ....
....
....

WEATHER (AM):	WEATHER (PM): ....
....	....
....	....
....	
AIR TEMP: WATER TEMP:	AIR TEMP: WATER TEMP:
....	....

SWIM:	RIG: ....
....	....
....	....

| NOTES: .... | MOON: ● ◖ ◗ ☾ ○ |

....
....
....
....

SPECIES	BAIT	TIME	WEIGHT	LENGTH	COMMENTS

SPECIES CAUGHT:

TOTAL FISH CAUGHT:

DATE: .... LOCATION: .... HOURS FISHED:

....

....

DAY: .... WATER: .... BEST TIMES: ....

....

....

PEOPLE FISHED WITH: ....

....

....

WEATHER (AM): .... WEATHER (PM): ....

....

....

....

AIR TEMP: WATER TEMP: AIR TEMP: WATER TEMP:

....

SWIM: .... RIG: ....

....

....

NOTES: ....   MOON: ●◖◗◑○

....

....

....

....

....

SPECIES	BAIT	TIME	WEIGHT	LENGTH	COMMENTS

SPECIES CAUGHT:

....

TOTAL FISH CAUGHT:

....

DATE: .... **LOCATION:** .... **HOURS FISHED:** ....

....

....

DAY: .... **WATER:** .... **BEST TIMES:** ....

....

....

PEOPLE FISHED WITH: ....

....

....

WEATHER (AM): .... **WEATHER (PM):** ....

....

....

....

AIR TEMP: **WATER TEMP:**   **AIR TEMP:**   **WATER TEMP:**

....

SWIM: .... **RIG:** ....

....

....

NOTES: .... **MOON:** ● ◐ ☽ ○

....

....

....

....

....

SPECIES	BAIT	TIME	WEIGHT	LENGTH	COMMENTS

SPECIES CAUGHT:
....

TOTAL FISH CAUGHT:
....

DATE: .... LOCATION: .... HOURS FISHED:
....
....

DAY: .... WATER: .... BEST TIMES: ....
....
....

PEOPLE FISHED WITH: ....
....
....

WEATHER (AM): .... WEATHER (PM): ....
....
....
....

AIR TEMP: WATER TEMP: AIR TEMP: WATER TEMP:
....

SWIM: .... RIG: ....
....
....

NOTES: .... MOON: ●◗◖◖🌙○
....
....
....
....

SPECIES	BAIT	TIME	WEIGHT	LENGTH	COMMENTS

SPECIES CAUGHT:

TOTAL FISH CAUGHT:

DATE: .... LOCATION: .... HOURS FISHED:
....
....

DAY: .... WATER: .... BEST TIMES: ....
....
....

PEOPLE FISHED WITH: ....
....
....

WEATHER (AM): .... WEATHER (PM): ....
....
....
....

AIR TEMP: WATER TEMP: AIR TEMP: WATER TEMP:
....

SWIM: .... RIG: ....
....
....

NOTES: .... MOON: ● ◗ ◖ ◖ ○
....
....
....
....
....

SPECIES	BAIT	TIME	WEIGHT	LENGTH	COMMENTS

SPECIES CAUGHT:

TOTAL FISH CAUGHT:

DATE:	LOCATION:	HOURS FISHED:
....	....	....
....	....	....
DAY:	WATER:	BEST TIMES: ....
....	....	....
....	....	....

PEOPLE FISHED WITH: ....
....
....

WEATHER (AM):	WEATHER (PM): ....
....	....
....	....
....	....
AIR TEMP: WATER TEMP:	AIR TEMP: WATER TEMP:
....	....

SWIM:	RIG: ....
....	....
....	....

NOTES: ....

MOON:

....
....
....
....
....

SPECIES	BAIT	TIME	WEIGHT	LENGTH	COMMENTS

SPECIES CAUGHT:

....

TOTAL FISH CAUGHT:

....

DATE:	LOCATION:	HOURS FISHED:
....	....	....
....	....	....
DAY:	WATER:	BEST TIMES: ....
....	....	....
....	....	....

PEOPLE FISHED WITH: ....
....
....

WEATHER (AM):	WEATHER (PM): ....
....	....
....	....
....	....
AIR TEMP: WATER TEMP:	AIR TEMP: WATER TEMP:
....	....

SWIM:	RIG: ....
....	....
....	....

| NOTES: .... | MOON: ● ◖ ◑ ◗ ○ |

....
....
....
....
....

SPECIES	BAIT	TIME	WEIGHT	LENGTH	COMMENTS

SPECIES CAUGHT:

TOTAL FISH CAUGHT:

DATE: .... | LOCATION: .... | HOURS FISHED: ....

DAY: .... | WATER: .... | BEST TIMES: ....

PEOPLE FISHED WITH: ....

WEATHER (AM): .... | WEATHER (PM): ....

AIR TEMP: WATER TEMP: | AIR TEMP: WATER TEMP:

SWIM: .... | RIG: ....

NOTES: .... | MOON: ◐ ◖ ◖ ◗ ○

SPECIES	BAIT	TIME	WEIGHT	LENGTH	COMMENTS

SPECIES CAUGHT:

TOTAL FISH CAUGHT:

DATE:	LOCATION:	HOURS FISHED:
....	....	....
....	....	....
DAY:	WATER:	BEST TIMES: ....
....	....	....
....	....	....

PEOPLE FISHED WITH: ....
....
....

WEATHER (AM):	WEATHER (PM): ....
....	....
....	....
....	....
AIR TEMP: WATER TEMP:	AIR TEMP: WATER TEMP:
....	....

SWIM:	RIG: ....
....	....
....	....

NOTES: ....   MOON: ● ◐ ◑ ☽ ○
....
....
....
....
....

SPECIES	BAIT	TIME	WEIGHT	LENGTH	COMMENTS

SPECIES CAUGHT:

TOTAL FISH CAUGHT:

DATE: .... | LOCATION: .... | HOURS FISHED:
.... | .... | ....
.... | .... | ....

DAY: .... | WATER: .... | BEST TIMES: ....
.... | .... | ....
.... | .... | ....

PEOPLE FISHED WITH: ....
....
....

WEATHER (AM): .... | WEATHER (PM): ....
.... | ....
.... | ....
.... | ....

AIR TEMP: WATER TEMP: | AIR TEMP: WATER TEMP:
.... | ....

SWIM: .... | RIG: ....
.... | ....
.... | ....

NOTES: .... | MOON: ● ◗ ◖ ☽ ○
....
....
....
....

SPECIES	BAIT	TIME	WEIGHT	LENGTH	COMMENTS

SPECIES CAUGHT:

TOTAL FISH CAUGHT:

DATE:	LOCATION:	HOURS FISHED:
....	....	....
....	....	....

DAY:	WATER:	BEST TIMES: ....
....	....	....
....	....	....

PEOPLE FISHED WITH: ....
....
....

WEATHER (AM):	WEATHER (PM): ....
....	....
....	....
....	....
AIR TEMP: WATER TEMP:	AIR TEMP: WATER TEMP:
....	....

SWIM:	RIG: ....
....	....
....	....

NOTES: ....
....
....
....
....

MOON: ◖◗◖◗◗ ○

SPECIES	BAIT	TIME	WEIGHT	LENGTH	COMMENTS

SPECIES CAUGHT:

....

TOTAL FISH CAUGHT:

....

DATE:	LOCATION:	HOURS FISHED:
....	....	....
DAY:	WATER:	BEST TIMES: ....
....	....	....

PEOPLE FISHED WITH: ....
....
....

WEATHER (AM):	WEATHER (PM): ....
....	....
AIR TEMP: WATER TEMP:	AIR TEMP: WATER TEMP: ....

| SWIM: .... | RIG: .... |
| ....
.... | ....
.... |

NOTES: ....

MOON:

....
....
....
....
....

SPECIES	BAIT	TIME	WEIGHT	LENGTH	COMMENTS

SPECIES CAUGHT:
....

TOTAL FISH CAUGHT:
....

DATE: .... | LOCATION: .... | HOURS FISHED:
.... | .... | ....
.... | .... | ....

DAY: .... | WATER: .... | BEST TIMES: ....
.... | .... | ....
.... | .... | ....

PEOPLE FISHED WITH: ....
....
....

WEATHER (AM): .... | WEATHER (PM): ....
.... | ....
.... | ....
.... | ....

AIR TEMP: WATER TEMP: | AIR TEMP: WATER TEMP:
.... | ....

SWIM: .... | RIG: ....
.... | ....
.... | ....

NOTES: .... | MOON: ● ☾ ☾ ☾ ○
....
....
....
....

SPECIES	BAIT	TIME	WEIGHT	LENGTH	COMMENTS

SPECIES CAUGHT:

....

TOTAL FISH CAUGHT:

....